GOSPILLS

A Daily Dose of God's Medicine for His Children

JEFF JOHNSON

WORD & SPIRIT
PUBLISHING

GOSPILLS
Copyright © 2017 by Jeff Johnson

ISBN: 978-1-949106-17-6

All Scripture quotations unless otherwise designated are taken from the King James Version (KJV) is public domain, and may be freely used.

Published by Word and Spirit Publishing
P.O. Box 701403
Tulsa, Oklahoma 74170
wordandspiritpublishing.com

Dedicated to my beautiful wife and best friend Kathleen. Life with you is better than lemon drops.

INTRODUCTION

*"For they (God's Words) are life and health
to all of your flesh"* (Proverbs 4:22).

The United States today makes up only five percent of the world's population, yet it consumes over half of the prescription medications manufactured worldwide. You do not have to watch television very long before you see a commercial for the latest pill being offered by big pharma, with it's promises to alleviate one of the many burdens that man faces daily in this fallen world. There seems to be a pill for every type of malady known to mankind.

I have spent the last eighteen years of my life working for two different generic drug manufacturers, and I believe in the power of many wonderful medicines that I have seen save and extend lives. I would be a hypocrite (even more of one than I am already) if I were to attack the drug industry or any of God's wonderful children that work within it's walls. I write these words to you today to share my life's real passion with you instead.

I have had the distinct privilege of sitting at the feet of Jesus over the past eleven years by simply starting each day opening His Word with my heart wide open, ready to hear Him speak to me. I have found that as I read and put His Word into practice by believing, speaking and acting on it, that it literally becomes active and alive like a medication. Simply put, God's Word has extremely active ingredients. I have seen countless lives (including mine) healed, restored, renewed, and revived by the living Word of God, received in faith and spoken in favor to anyone willing to believe. I have been blessed beyond measure by God as He has helped me step by step to become fully persuaded that what He has promised, He is able to perform (Romans 4:21).

The Bible says repeatedly that God is no respecter of persons (Romans 2:11) so I believe that what I have experienced through God's Word is available to each and every one of His children. I write these words down for you, Child of God, in hopes that you will see even greater things as you open your heart to the Lord. I want to share some basic truths with you about how to ingest God's Word like a daily medicine, as I know and believe it will bring life and health to your mind and body. I believe with all my heart that God's Word is the best medicine that you can ever take, and it's side effects include love, joy, peace, patience, kindness, goodness, faithfulness, gentleness, and self-control.

Since most medicines today are taken over a thirty-day period, I would like to invite you to take a thirty-day prescription of God's Word with me starting right now. The key with any good medicine is to take one pill at a time, giving each dose it's time to sink into your being and release its power according to the manufacturer's instructions. God has always intended for His Children to live life one day at a time, and He promises only the strength and provision required for each day. All you need today is one verse, one word from God to sink into your Spirit, Soul, and Body, and you will see His power manifest itself in you. Since Jesus is often called the Great Physician, I had Him write you a prescription for a thirty-day dose of His Gospills and hope that you enjoy taking the medicine of His Holy Word.

PRESCRIPTION

NAME _____ AGE _____
ADDRESS _____ DATE _____

Indications: Taking this medication will help you to become fully convinced of the accuracy, reliability, and integrity of God's Holy Word.

Recommended Dosage: Take one Gospill per day for a thirty-day period.

Warning: Becoming fully convinced that all scripture is God breathed will give you bold Bible faith that conquers and overcomes all challenges you face each day.

_____   **The Great Physician**
Date   Doctor's Name

GOSPILL 1

"All Scripture is God-breathed and is useful for teaching, rebuking, correcting and training in Righteousness, so that the man of God may be thoroughly equipped for every good work" (2 Timothy 3:16–17).

Today's verse is the starting point for any person desiring bold Bible faith, who wants to see the power of God manifest in their lives. You must be fully established in the fact that all scripture is inspired by God. Like any work of the Holy Spirit, this comes by revelation, which comes by seeking truth and asking the Lord to reveal it to you. Over the years, I have become more and more convinced that God's Word really is active and alive and sharper than any two edged sword (Hebrews 4:12). There is no person on this earth who can convince me that God's Word is manmade, simply because I have seen its power work in my life and the lives of others over and over again. I have seen countless people in my circle of influence get healed of diseases, set free from depression and delivered from addiction. Lately, most of these people have been nonbelievers, who were desperate enough to reach through this crowded world and touch the hem of Jesus's garment to receive their healing. Once you receive Jesus as healer, or deliverer, you can then trust Him and receive Him as a friend or brother as well. You see, once something works in your life, there won't be any person who can convince you that it doesn't. I often tell people who refuse to believe and who try to convince me that God's Word is not reliable: "Your too late, God's Word (Jesus) is already working in my life." Work out your own salvation today by saying, "Lord, I choose to believe you, I choose to take you at your Word."

Today's Prayer: Father God, today I choose to believe that you gave your Word to each, and every person who chooses Jesus as Lord and Savior. I ask for the power of your Holy Spirit to reveal to me the truth about your Word. I thank you that you have spoken in your Word today as I have felt my heart burning with truth. Help these seeds of faith in your Word go deep down into the soil of my heart and let them grow like a mighty oak tree. In Jesus's Name. Amen.

GOSPILL 2

"For the word of God is living and active. Sharper than any double-edged sword, it penetrates even to dividing soul and spirit, joints and marrow; it judges the thoughts and attitudes of the heart" (Hebrews 4:12).

Today's dose of God's Word is one of my favorites. I not only believe in it's complete accuracy, but I have been blessed to see it actually go to work on countless individuals including myself. I have seen my friend, Jeff, recently healed of heart disease by the Word of God and seen my uncle healed of cancer by that same Word. I have seen backs healed and bones mended, depression defeated, and souls set on fire simply through applying God's Word to each and every situation that this world can throw at you.

Applying God's Word to your life is as simple as hearing the Word (through your ears, in your heart) having faith come alive in you and then applying the Word to your situation by speaking it out of your mouth. We are instructed by Jesus to speak His Word to our mountain (mountain of cancer, mountain of depression, mountain of debt etc.) and we are promised that mountain will move (Mark 11:23). God's Word says that we can bless (or curse) with our words, and so we apply God's Word liberally as we curse cancer and bless the body from which it is removed. We speak God's Word in the name of Jesus, for through Him authority is given to the believer. When we believe that the Holy Spirit is in us and on us to do these works, we can boldly claim God's Word over our lives and the lives of those close to us and rely on the name of Jesus to back it up (John 14:12).

It's time to take God quite literally at His Word. When He says we can do something in His name, we can do it (Mark 16:17–18). When He says we have His power to back us then we believe we have it (Philippians 4:13) and so we speak it out into the atmosphere and see the Word go to work!

Prayer: Father, today I believe and receive your Word with childlike simplicity. Faith is simple; you have made it that way. We can believe and receive, or doubt and do without! From this day forward I choose to believe in your Word and in the name of

Jesus as my authority to back it up! I expect to see miracles abound, and faith explode like never before in Jesus's name. Amen!

GOSPILL 3

"And the Word was made flesh, and dwelt among us, (and we beheld His glory, the glory as of the only begotten of the Father,) full of grace and truth" (John 1:14).

It's absolutely amazing to see that Jesus *is* the Word of God wrapped in human flesh. Jesus is the embodiment of God's Holy Word. I like to refer to Him as a walkie-talkie. In His short three-year ministry on earth, He walked, talked, and put into action the Word of God; He made the Word come alive. I know that I don't have the proper words to describe this, nor do I have a full understanding of its implications, but it's so wonderful none the less.

Jesus told us also that when we see Him, we are seeing the Father (John 14:7) which is amazing because The God that most of the church portrays today looks nothing like Jesus. The Bible sums up Jesus's entire ministry (Acts 10:38) by saying that Jesus went about doing good and healing *all* (that word in Greek means all) that were sick and oppressed by the devil, because God was with Him. Jesus healed all, not some, but all. He never spoke of sickness as having some "divine purpose" or some twisted "will of the Father" He simply saw it for what it was, evil, and eradicated it by His Word.

Jesus calls us today to see Him in the gospels as the Word of God personified, speaking words of life, touching the sick and depressed, feeding the hungry, and helping any and all that come across His path. He now sits in Heaven at the Father's right hand and *has sent* us believers His Holy Spirit to allow us to do the same things He did and more (John 14:12). He commands us to heal the sick, cleanse the diseased, to cast out evil spirits because as He *has given* us freely of His Spirit, He expects us to freely give it back to those in need (Matthew 10:8). I know that most churches do not teach this today, but I am here to tell you plainly what is contained in His Word. His Church today is not powerless, but powerful in Him. I call you today to see Christ *in you* (Colossians 1:27) and step out in faith and do the things He has called you to do. When Jesus commands the impossible, He then makes the impossible possible *through us* (Matthew 19:26)!

Prayer: Father God, thank you for sending Jesus so we could see your Holy Word personified. Thank you for sending us your Holy Spirit to empower us to do the same things Jesus did, these same things He calls us to do today. We believe and receive by the faith of Jesus, your presence, and power to take the first step and we delight to see you working through us today!

GOSPILL 4

"But He answered and said, it is written, Man shall not live by bread alone, but by every word that proceeds out of the mouth of God" (Matthew 4:4).

I love this scripture because it reminds us that Jesus had the ultimate reverence for the Word of God. Even though He was the Word personified, He taught us to use the power and authority of His Word to whip the devil at every turn. He literally swung the two-edged Sword of the Word of God (by speaking it) and hit the devil with several mighty blows all preceded by Him saying, "It is written, it is written, it is written!" Throughout the Gospels Jesus is constantly quoting scripture, showing us how to skillfully train ourselves with God's only offensive weapon, the mighty double-edged sword of His Word.

Since the only thing that pleases God is faith (Hebrews 11:6) and we know faith comes by hearing God's Word (Romans 10:17), we can easily see why the enemy's main focus is to damage our faith by stealing the seed of God's Word (Mark 4) before it can grow. The enemy comes to steal, kill, and destroy (John 10:10), and he does this by trying to steal, kill, and destroy your faith. His main mission today is stealing the seeds that we find in the Word of God (Mark 4) because they are the very thing that produces a harvest of faith. The enemy has no power to just kill a believer, if he did none of us would be alive. What he tries to do is damage the credibility of God's Word by saying the same thing he said to Adam and Eve in the garden, "Did God really say that?" As we read God's Word more and more we see that every word is Good News and the enemy's last tactic is to make us question it's reliability and integrity. Settle it in your heart today; God's Word is 100 percent accurate, reliable, and powerful. It's active ingredient (what makes it work) is faith. Simply put, you can believe and receive His promises contained in His Word, or you can doubt and do without.

I call you today to draw a line in the sand and make up your mind once and for all that God's Word is accurate, reliable, and powerful for those who mix it with faith. His Word is strong medicine for those who take it with faith, and it can literally move mountains if you allow it to.

Prayer: Heavenly Father, I thank you for your Holy Word today! I settle in my heart once and for all that your Word is accurate, reliable, and powerful. From this day forth I promise to take you at your Word. I ask you to show me your will by teaching me your Word. Thank you Holy Spirit for convincing me that your Word is your will and your will is your Word. I receive today the incorruptible seed of your Word, planted deep into my heart, and I thank you for fertilizing it with faith and watering it with living water. I take up my sword and wield it with faith. Amen!

GOSPILL 5

"Sanctify them through thy truth: thy word is truth" (John 17:17).

Today's Gospill is a seed that comes from Jesus's final prayer to the Father on behalf of all believers, both at that present moment and all those that would follow. This is very exciting because this prayer was made to carry throughout eternity. It is an ever-present prayer prayed by Jesus for you and me! Hallelujah! It's also a prayer for anyone who will believe on Jesus through our sharing of the gospel (John 17:20).

Jesus is asking the Father to sanctify us through His truth, which is His Word, which as we know is also Jesus' Himself. The word "Sanctify" here means to consecrate, to set apart, and to make Holy. Jesus is asking the Father to make us Holy by knowing Him through His Word. The Father wants us to know Him by knowing Jesus in our born again Spirit. We no longer are to regard Him as flesh and blood, but are to commune with Him through His Spirit which is sealed in us (2 Corinthians 5:16–17). We worship and commune with God through the power and operation of the Holy Spirit in us (1 Corinthians 6:17). Any believer who reads His Bible knows that it's no ordinary book. God's Words on those pages are Spirit and Life (John 6:63) because they were spoken out of the same mouth that spoke the heavens and earth into being. Hallelujah!

I ask you again today, to let this seed of thought get deep down into the soil of your soul. Settle it in your heart once and for all that God was able to compile sixty-six books of scripture, which we call our Bible, in order to give us instruction in how to live in the Spirit. Remember, we are now to identify ourselves as Spirit beings and not according to our Flesh, that is our mind and body (Philippians 3:3). You are *not* a physical being; you are a spirit who possesses a soul and lives in a body. Let God's Word reveal to you today who *you are* in your spirit, and don't give any thought to your dead flesh (Romans 8:10).

Prayer: Father God, thank you for Jesus! Thank you for His sacrifice which nailed my old sin nature to the cross and gave me His new righteous nature in exchange. I stand before your throne today in right standing with you because of Jesus. All glory and praise goes to Him for His finished work, which I receive by faith today. Thank you for allowing me to walk in this newness of life today, and for letting the light of Christ shine on every single person who enters my circle of grace today. I let go and let you flow through me today by your Holy Spirit who has made His home in me. Thank you for allowing me to see how good the Good News really is! It's beyond what I imagined and I can't thank you enough! I love you Lord! Amen.

GOSPILL 6

"By The Word of the Lord were the heavens made, and all the host of them by the breath of His mouth" (Psalm 33:6).

This verse shows us the remarkable power of God's Word. The truth that God actually spoke the world into existence really blesses me big time! When I consider that we are created in His image (Genesis 1:27) and He has made us the only species that can speak words, I am in awe to consider the power of His Word and our words.

Everyone (even lost people) know how badly words can either wound or bless people in their lives. Perhaps someone spoke words of hurt over you when you were young, and those words still hang over you today. We truly get to decide what words we speak to each other every day. God says that He sets before us each day the choice to speak words of life or death over each other, and implores us to always choose life (Deuteronomy 30:19). We are encouraged as believers to speak God's Word over each other with the strength and power that the Holy Spirit provides (1 Peter 4:11). God further promises us as we step out in faith behind His Word that His power will be there to make the things in the Spirit realm manifest themselves in this fallen world. We can literally speak His kingdom down from Heaven by the bridge of faith and see His Will/Word being done here in the natural (Matthew 6:10).

We use words each and every day to build our world here on earth. Words can start wars or heal wounds, the choice lies with each individual. Once you begin to plant the seed of God's Word in your heart, you will find that His Words begin to flow from your lips with ease and the people around you will know that you have been spending time with the Lord (Acts 4:13). Yes, His Word says that He has given our tongue the power of life and death (Proverbs 18:21), and we ask the Holy Spirit today to move in us as we choose life. His Word says that our words will actually set our whole world on fire (James 3) either with the Holy Spirit's fire of faith and love or the devil's fire of fear and hate. May the words of your mouth and the meditation of your heart be pleasing to the Lord today (Psalm 19:14).

Prayer: Father, I ask you today to reveal Your Word to me, reveal Jesus in me, and let the words of my mouth be sweet like honey, seasoned with grace so that those who hear can be blessed and edified by them. Thank you for giving me words of life that can bless those who step inside my circle today. Thank you for putting a guard over my mouth to help me watch my words and thereby bless you. In Jesus's name I pray. Amen.

GOSPILL 7

"If ye abide in me and my words abide in you, ye shall ask what ye will and it shall be done unto you" (John 15:7).

This verse really blessed me this morning because God confirms, once again, that His Word is His Will. We spend so much time as Christians wondering what God's Will is for our lives. Look no further than His Word and you will find His Will. His Will for you, His Will for the world, His Will for your family, His Will for your friends etcetera, etcetera. Faith is simple, it comes by hearing God's Word/Will (Romans 10:17).

The even greater news is that once we start to believe and to take God at His Word, we can begin to pray according to His Word and therefore can bring the things of Heaven down to earth. This isn't crazy, that's what Jesus said when He taught us the

Lord's Prayer. He said to our Father in heaven, your will (word) be done on earth as it is done in Heaven (Matthew 6:10). Pray according to His Word, and you will pray according to His will. If you are worried about old age, then pray "With long life God will satisfy me and show me His Salvation" (Psalm 91:16). If you are worried about your finances say out loud, "My God shall supply all my needs according to His glorious riches in Christ Jesus" (Philippians 4:19). If you are facing a health crisis pray, "By the stripes of Jesus, I declare myself healed" (Isaiah 53:5, 1 Peter 2:24). This is so simple; you have to hire a theologian to help you to complicate it. God has always wanted us to keep things simple (2 Corinthians 11:3) from day one in The Garden of Eden all the way to your Garden today. You are God's Garden, and He is planting the seed of His Word in you every day from this day forward (1 Peter 1:23).

Prayer: Father God, thank you for revealing to me this morning/evening by your Holy Spirit, that your Word is reliable and trustworthy! Thank you for teaching me to pray according to your will, which is your Word, and for assuring me that I already have these petitions that I desire of you. Thank you for revealing your presence in me today so that I can fill up on your love and devotion to the point of overflow! Now let me go and pour your living water on some thirsty soul today! In Jesus's name, I seal this prayer with a holy kiss! Amen!

GOSPILL 8

> *"Neither have I gone back from the commandments of His lips; I have esteemed the words of His mouth more than my necessary food"* (Job 23:12).

Today's daily dose of God's Word really speaks to us about the necessity of hearing from God through His Holy Word. We have already established and believe that ALL scripture is inspired by God and is spoken to us, His children. Job knew full well that God's Word was His Spiritual daily bread. Jesus Himself said that His food was to do the Will/Word of His Father (John 4:34) and that this was more important by far than physical food.

My heart is jumping with joy this morning as I look back over the past eleven years. I am reminded of all the times God met me in the early hours of the morning to speak with me through His precious Word. If there is one thing I would like to impress upon you, if I could give you my most prized possession, it is this: take time each morning to sit quietly with the Lord and open up your heart to His Word and start a dialogue with Him. It's a 100 percent iron clad guarantee that God will show up and speak to your heart/spirit and commune with you. If Jesus Himself had to sneak away from the crowds and find a quiet place to commune with our Father, then how much more do we need to do the same? I am telling you that I would not be alive today if not for these precious morning times that I have devoted to the Lord. I actually get excited each morning to sit down with my coffee and my Bible and begin an inward and outward dialogue with my Lord and Savior!

God's Word is Spirit and it *is life* (John 6:63), and it really is active and full of life (Hebrews 4:12). You can take my word for this, but better yet, take God at His Word. Real Love affords us free will, so you will have to choose whether or not you give these morning devotional times their well-deserved priority in your life. I hope and pray that you seek the Lord each morning and see that His desire is to walk and talk with you in the cool of the garden, and that when you give Him the first fruits of your day, you will reap a harvest throughout the entire day!

Prayer: Father, I ask you in the name of Jesus, please give me a desire to commune with you each morning. Please let your Word come to life in me and let me see that Jesus is with me always and forever. Teach me and guide me in this life as I open up my heart to your Holy Word and begin to hear from you like never before. Help me to make this such a wonderful habit, that I can say, like Job, "I esteem your words more than my necessary food." Amen!

GOSPILL 9

"Keep this book of the law always on your lips; meditate on it day and night, so that you may be careful to do everything written in it. Then you will be prosperous and successful" (Joshua 1:8).

Praise God for His Word being simple and straight-forward! Even though this is an Old Testament scripture, written before Jesus established the New Covenant, it speaks to us today as strongly as the day it was written. Believers in Jesus, we are blessed to be under the New Covenant law of grace (Romans 6:14), love (Matthew 13:34), and faith (Romans 3:27), and therefore do not have to worry about keeping God's law to the exact letter. We instead can go by the instruction of God's Word through the guidance and leadership of His Holy Spirit who now resides inside us (2 Corinthians 3:6) to teach us to walk in love. When we are led by God's Spirit of Love, the natural result of this in our lives is the keeping of both the Old and New Testament laws by our new nature. In other words, when we love our neighbor, we will not steal from him or lie to him, and if we love our spouses, we would never consider cheating on them. By the Spirit we naturally keep *all* of the Ten Commandments and more (Romans 13:8–10) by walking in our new spiritual nature!

I love this scripture because it reminds us how important it is not only to hear and believe God's Word but to speak it out loud each day, or as the verse says keep it on our lips. I love driving in my car and speaking out God's Word over my life and the lives of people in need. I don't think the driver in the car next to me even knows what I am doing; they probably just think I am talking hands free on my cell phone (LOL). There is such power in the spoken Word of God on our lips that the Bible reminds us that death and life are in the power of our tongue (Proverbs 18:21). I encourage you today, to take just one verse that you like and speak it out loud and receive it for yourself. Once you learn to see, believe and speak God's Word, you will soon see the actual manifestation (answering of prayer) in your natural world. By meditating on God's Word you will become powerful and you will actually see the things of Heaven come down to earth on the bridge of your faith.

Prayer: Father God, in the name of Jesus I come to you this morning and give you thanks for the revelation of the power of your Word. I thank you for convincing me that your Word will never return void, and will always accomplish the things that it promises (Isaiah 55:11, Romans 4:21). I speak your Word out loud today with confidence and boldness and with faith in your goodness, so that I can have great expectations as I wait to see your Word come to life! Amen.

GOSPILL 10

"So is my Word that goes out from my mouth: it will not return to me empty, but will accomplish what I desire and achieve the purpose for which I sent it" (Isaiah 55:11).

I am so thankful to the Lord for showing me recently how powerful our words are. Both words of faith and words of fear will do their work in our lives. Of that you can be sure. It doesn't take any more energy to speak words of life, words that line up with the Word of God, than it does to speak negative words of death. I ask the Lord each day to *let the words of my mouth and the thoughts of my heart be pleasing to Him* (Psalm 19:14). Today's Gospill is so clear, that God's Word is never spoken in vain. He has given us His Word so that we can order our conversation right (Psalm 50:23), and He has promised that when we order our speech in line with His, then He shows us (manifests) His Salvation. When we speak words of life we actually release ministering Angels who rush to our earthly scene with great power to deliver us (Psalm 103:20).

I am reminded this morning that the Nation of Israel wandered around the desert for forty years searching for God's Promised Land, all the while they marched they spewed negative words of doubt, unbelief, and ingratitude. A journey that should have taken them a few days took them forty years as they were blinded and bound by the very words of their mouth. God called them a gainsaying people (Romans 10:21). That word gainsaying means to speak against or to oppose. They spoke against the promises of God and brought forty years of suffering upon themselves. All of their troubles were tongue troubles, just as all of our troubles are tongue troubles.

I implore you today to read James chapter 3 and see how powerful your tongue can be, both for good or evil. God spoke the world into existence and has created us in His image, so we can do the same thing. We literally speak our own world into existence. I know that most people don't want to hear this, but I am telling you that from this day forward you can literally start speaking life into your atmosphere, you can speak words of encouragement to those around you and you can speak words of praise to our wonderful God! God says that when we order our conversation right, He will show (manifest) His Salvation to us (Psalm 50:23). This makes me so excited about putting my words in line with His Word and seeing Jesus go to work in and around us!

Prayer: Father, put a guard over my mouth today and let me speak words that are pleasing to you. Let me bless and not curse. Holy Spirit, thank you for giving me the words to speak today and for allowing me to see that my words have power to move mountains. Amen!

GOSPILL 11

"Now ye are clean through the word which I have spoken to you" (John 15:3).

The cleansing that Jesus speaks about in this passage is a cleansing that works from the inside out. His Word cleanses our hearts/minds and moves outward into our body making it full of light and life (Matthew 6:22). His Word is life and health to all of our mind and body (Proverbs 4:22). Taking a bath is great (and greatly encouraged), but soaking in God's Word each day brings eternal cleansing by renewing our minds to think the way God thinks. More simply put, it keeps us thinking on good things (Philippians 4:8).

God tells us that the only thing that pleases Him, the only thing He is looking for in all the earth is faith (Hebrews 11:6). He is clear that He will reward those of us who open up His Word and seek

Him with all their heart. He literally shows up every time we seek Him. As we learn to hear Him speaking through His Word each day we become hooked on His presence and soon find that there is nothing else in this world that we desire more. Fellowshipping with the Lord each day brings us back to the garden where God originally intended us to dwell. Yes, God created us for relationship with Him, and as this relationship develops we can effortlessly share Him with others who can experience His Joy.

We often witness because we think that is what pleases God, but that is actually not true at all. He actually longs to have a relationship with us as Friend, Father, Brother, Counselor etc., etc. Having real fellowship with the Lord will cause us to walk in the Spirit by our new nature and do those things (like witnessing) that His Spirit desires. Yes, when we become one with Him, we actually get the desires of His heart, a heart we share with Him (Psalm 37:4).

Anyone who attempts to set aside time with the Lord each morning will experience a great resistance to this in their flesh. The Bible says that the mind of the natural man (our old nature) is at war with our *spirit mind* (new nature) and the two can never get along (Romans 8:7). The only solution is to renew your mind in God's Word and let the new computer program Jesus 7.0 take over your operating system by deleting the old man 1.0 system. This choice is ours; we have to let this mind which is in Christ be also in us (Philippians 2:5). You will have to fight this good fight of faith yourself (1 Timothy 6:12).

Prayer: Father, please lead me by your Holy Spirit and reveal Jesus in my heart and mind and help me to renew my mind daily so that I can think on good things all day like you do. Amen!

GOSPILL 12

"This is the covenant that I will make with them after those days, saith the Lord, I will put my laws into their hearts, and in their minds will I write them; and their sins and iniquities I will remember no more" (Hebrews 10:16–17).

Today's modern world is all about downloads. We download all kinds of content (words) onto our laptops and Smartphones, whether it is an e-book, music or game. Today's passage reminds me that God gives us an upload instead of a download. He *has* written His Word on our hearts/minds and when we meditate on it we are more or less "uploading" His thoughts into our soul/mind of our own free will. We are choosing to let His thoughts become our thoughts. Thoughts which are more than good, they are God (John 6:63). Truly the only thing better than thinking good thoughts is thinking God thoughts.

Everything we do in life starts with a thought. We think something, then we talk about it and eventually we act on it. Thoughts are seeds which grow up in us and cause us to do good or to do evil. The more we think about what God is thinking about, the more we start speaking and acting like children of God. Just as we inherit the physical traits of our earthly fathers through genetics, we inherit the Spiritual traits of our Father through His Word. When we find ourselves in one of life's pickles we can always say, "I wonder what my Father would think about this." We can then go to His Word and see and say what He is seeing and saying. This is exactly what Jesus did during His short time on earth. He always said that He was just saying what our Father told Him to say and doing what our Father told Him to do. Now that He has ascended into heaven and sent us His Holy Spirit, we can do the same things today.

I praise God that your heart is burning with God's truth as you read this devotional. I am blessed and reassured by God at this very moment that you are beginning to see with eyes of faith that God's Word is His will and His will is His Word. I am thankful that the Holy Spirit is reassuring you that you can completely rely on God's Word as accurate and true and that you can walk in His Word all the way through this life and into eternity (1 Peter 1:25).

Prayer: Father God, thank you for your Word. Thank you for sending Jesus who was Your Word made flesh (John 1:14). Thank you for your Holy Spirit that is bearing witness that I am now One Spirit with you (1 Corinthians 6:17) and that I can do all things through the Spirit of Christ which lives and abides in me forever (Philippians 4:13). I praise you and thank you for showing me that I can walk and talk with you all day long and learn to listen to your still, small voice which leads me and guides me to do your will. You are to be forever praised. Amen.

GOSPILL 13

"The Spirit gives life; the flesh counts for nothing. The words I have spoken to you are spirit and they are life" (John 6:63).

As born again believers, God makes it very clear that He no longer regards us according to our flesh (2 Corinthians 5:16). If you have not been born again, I encourage you today to ask the Lord Jesus into your heart, and He will gladly give you the free gift of the Holy Spirit. It's only with His presence and guidance that we can understand the scriptures. All scriptures were breathed by the Spirit of God working through mortal men and given to us for inspiration and instruction in Righteous living through Jesus (2 Timothy 3:16). God is no respecter of persons (Romans 2:11) so His free gift of His Holy Spirit is available to anyone who asks and receives Him as Lord.

Once you begin to see that you are One Spirit with the Lord (1 Corinthians 6:17) and that you are now adopted into the family of God, things really begin to change around you and through you. Once you begin to see who you are in the Spirit, and what rights and privileges you possess, life takes on a whole new meaning. I wish I had the words to describe what Jesus did for us at the cross of Calvary. He took our place on the cross and received our punishment and gave us (in a divine exchange) His Righteous Spirit (2 Corinthians 5:21). God now sees us as New Creatures in the Spirit of Christ (2 Corinthians 5:17) and no longer regards us according to our flesh (John 4:24). He has always longed to commune with us in Spirit, and now through the finished work of Jesus Christ we have that ability and most high privilege.

We were naturally born into this world through the corrupted seed of Adam, and have now been born again through the incorruptible seed of the Word of God–(1 Peter 1:23). We have been reborn spiritually and can now commune with God the way He originally intended (see John 4:23–24). Jesus has adorned you with His Robe of Righteousness and when the Father looks at you, He sees you wrapped in His Son and says, "With you I am well pleased." This news is almost too good to be true. That is exactly what the word gospel means in Greek, nearly too good to be true news.

Prayer: Father God, help me to see who I am right now in my born again Spirit. Thank you for giving me the boldness of a lion to believe and receive what Christ has provided for me through His perfect work on the cross. Let me receive by His faith what has already been provided and help me today to walk in this newness of life, as I walk in the Spirit with you today! Amen

GOSPILL 14

"You show that you are a letter from Christ, the result of our ministry, written not with ink but with the Spirit of the living God, not on tablets of stone but on the tablets of human hearts" (2 Corinthians 3:3).

I'm sure that you have heard the saying that you may be the only Bible that certain people might ever read. This statement, as we can see above, is very scriptural and very true. When you open God's Word, you open your heart and are able to see that what He has already written on your heart is reflected on the pages and vice versa (Hebrews 8:10). Once we start to upload His Word from our heart (Spirit) to our head (our soul/mind) we begin to change.

God's Word is designed to show you who you are in Christ now that you have been reborn (born again) of His Spirit. His Word is designed to show you that you have been made Righteous through the finished work of Jesus Christ. His Word shows you that a great exchange took place at The Cross of Calvary. Jesus took your sin (past, present and future) and gave you His Righteousness (right standing with God) as a free gift (2 Corinthians 5:21). When you accept this free gift you are set free to live a new life in His Spirit and in His Spirit is no sin (1 John 3:9). As you freely receive from God, freely you can give to others through His Spirit in you and then the Lord can set others free as well.

It is imperative that we believers begin to operate in the gifts God has assigned to each of us. Gifts of faith, healing, wisdom, miracles, discernment, and encouragement (1 Corinthians 12) have been given to each of us, and we are to operate in these gifts for the benefit of every child of God. We always give first to the family of faith and then to those who we are inviting into the family (Galatians 6:10). I believe that God is calling us believers into our prayer closets and out into The World to walk in the Spirit and do just as Jesus did while he walked the earth (Mark 16:17–18). We are to lay hands on the sick, cast out evil spirits and work with signs that show the world that we have the backing and authority of God in the name of Jesus. I believe that in these last days believers will be called forward to minister as Jesus did or they will be called up if they refuse to operate in The Power that God has provided. They will not be able to overcome the enemy without knowing and operating in the power and authority that Jesus has gifted to us by His Holy Spirit.

Prayer: Father let us go boldly today into this world and show them Jesus moving in us! Amen.

GOSPILL 15

"Blessed are they which do hunger and thirst after Righteousness: for they shall be filled" (Matthew 5:6).

Blessed are you right now because you are reading this devotional. Only a person who is hungry for Righteousness would read and meditate on The Word of God. The word Righteousness simply means "Right Standing" with God. When we look to Jesus and His finished work on the cross, we begin to see and experience our own personal "Right Standing" with God that has been provided to us as a free gift. The more God reveals our Righteousness in Christ to us, the more free we feel on the inside, and the more free we feel on the inside, the more we show it on the outside.

If you have made Jesus your Lord and Savior, you will never be more righteous than you are right now at this very moment. Jesus took your sin and gave you His Righteousness when He gave you His life. You are forever Righteous in the eyes of The Father, because when He looks at you He sees the Spirit of His Son in you. He no longer sees sin, He sees His Son (Hebrews 10:17). As far as the east is from the west, that is how far He *has* removed your sins from you (Psalm 103:12).

As believers, we want to spend each day learning a little bit more about our rights and privileges that His gift of Righteousness affords to us. We can go to school each day by using His Word to instruct us in Righteousness (2 Timothy 3:16) so that we can honor God by partaking in all that Christ has provided for us. Most believers today (myself included) live well below the poverty line when it comes to partaking in our right-standing with God. We most often believe for very little and that is exactly what we experience. We aim at nothing and hit it every time!

Today is the day that we turn things around by simply taking God at His Word. We are who His Word says we are, and we have what His Word says we have! We say with confidence and boldness: God said it, I believe it; that settles it!

Prayer: Father God, help us today to start believing big. Let us come to your table every day hungry and thirsty for the free gift of Righteousness that you have provided through your Son's finished work on the cross. Let our faith that we share in Him, the faith of your Spirit in us come alive. Let us see with open eyes and open hearts what is the length and height and depth of the love you have for us in Christ Jesus. Fill our cups to overflow today Father! Amen

GOSPILL 16

"For this is the covenant that I will make with the house of Israel after those days, saith the Lord: I will put my laws into their mind, and write them in their hearts: and I will be their God and they will be my people: and they shall not teach every man his neighbor, and every man his brother, saying Know the Lord: for all shall know me, from the least to the greatest" (Hebrews 8:10).

Lord, I love what you are showing us this morning. You have written your Holy Word on our heart (spirit) which is why the truth of these scriptures makes our heart jump with joy when we see them.

According to this verse, it is now the desire of God to teach every man about Jesus on a very personal level. We rely way too much today on people that we believe to be "more spiritual" than the rest of us. Most often it is someone like our Pastor, or a Missionary friend or some other "full time Christian." This is a burden that God never intended for them (or for us) to bear. God's desire is to speak to each of us privately throughout the day in a way that is unique to each and every one of us. Only God knows the intimate details of your life from the inside out. He knows ahead of time who will cross your path today, and He knows exactly how to reach that person through you. He has made you so unique in giving you a fingerprint that no one else possesses and DNA that can only be traced back to you. He knows that only you were designed to reach the people that step inside your circle of influence today. No one else was designed like you. You were designed to fulfill the specific purpose He has for your life.

I implore you in The Name of Jesus to see how special you are right now at this very moment. You are God's workmanship created in Christ Jesus to do the good works He has planned for you alone (Ephesians 2:10). You have the Spirit of Christ in you, the very same power that raised Jesus from the dead is in you forever (Ephesians 1:19). God's ability and your availability today are a dynamite combination, and the Holy Spirit is about to explode in your circle today. Anyone who crosses your path today better get ready for a super-natural encounter with God. His "Super" and your "Natural" are like peas and carrots, like Forest and Jenny.

Prayer: Father God, thank you for teaching me your Word (Jesus) today! Thank you for giving me awareness at all times that Christ Jesus resides in me by your Holy Spirit and for giving me the power to walk on water when I step out of my boat today. Thank you for the Love and compassion that you have poured into my heart (Romans 5:5) so that whoever crosses my path today will know that Jesus is alive, and He lives to love them. Amen!

GOSPILL 17

"Heaven and earth shall pass away: but my words shall not pass away" (Luke 21:33).

I thank God every day for the integrity and complete reliability of His Holy Word! When you begin to build your life on God's Word, you become that wise man who built his house on a solid foundation instead of sinking sand (Matthew 7:24). When you put God's Word to work in your life by praying it and speaking it into your atmosphere, you can be 100 percent certain that you will see it manifest in ways that you never imagined. Simply put, God's Words are Spirit, and they are life (John 6:63).

Day in and day out, we rely on so many people in this world and things in this world to make us happy and whole. But people let us down, and things rust and fade away. Have you tried to rely on what God says will make you happy and whole? Have you thought about what it means to believe in Jesus Christ and to make Him your Lord and Savior? Jesus says that once we know how much He loves us and how much He cares for us, that we should find it easy to do what He says (John 14:15). His Word contains His Will for our lives, and His Word shows us who we are in Him and what great power and authority we possess as believers. These facts alone should cause our hearts to leap and sing when we see and hear The Word of God spoken over us daily (John 15:3).

I implore you today to make God's Word the cornerstone of your life. Build your life and the life of your family on God's eternal Word, because His Word is the only thing that lasts forever. Jesus is The Word of God made flesh and now as believers we too are The Word of God, walking and talking to this dying world by His Spirit that lives in us (1 Corinthians 3:16). We are the only Bible that a lot of people will ever see or read (2 Corinthians 3:3) and so we must have God's Words of encouragement flowing out of our lips each day to bring light and life to so many souls lost in darkness. Jesus said that while He was in the world that He was the light of The World (John 9:5). But He also says that we are The Light of the world (Matthew 5:14) by His Spirit living in us and through us to touch those in need around us. I am asking you to simply believe what His Word says and then boldly step out of your boat and onto the water.

Prayer: Father God, thank you for showing me a little bit more of who I am in Christ and what I possess as your child. Help me by the power of your Holy Spirit to see Jesus in me and to act according to Your Word. Speak to me each moment and guide me through this life. Use me today as your instrument of Righteousness and help me to honor and act as the child of God that Jesus has made me. Thank you for giving me everything that I need in life by giving me your Holy Spirit to lead me and guide me as I walk out Your Word today. Amen!

GOSPILL 18

"So then faith comes by hearing, and hearing by the word of the Lord" (Romans 10:17).

The Bible clearly states that without faith it is impossible to please God (Hebrews 11:6). In order to see God's presence manifest in your life you must first believe that He exists, and that He rewards those that seek Him diligently (Hebrews 11:6). Throughout The Gospels, we see that Jesus was constantly looking for faith and faith alone. He praised a heathen for having the greatest faith He had ever seen (Matthew 8:10) and rebuked St. Peter for having such little faith (Matthew 14:31). God really is no respecter of persons, He only digs faith!

So the questions we all ask is this: If faith is what pleases God, then how do I get more of it? Today's verse makes the answer plain and simple. We increase our faith by increasing our knowledge of God's Word. Faith comes by hearing over and over again the three-thousand-plus promises God has made to His Children in the Holy Bible, His last will and testament to His kids. We hear The Word coming into our ears through good and true Grace preaching and we hear God speak to us in our heart/spirit when we read His Word in silence and listen for His still, small voice. You can mark my words, once you start to fill yourself each day with His Word, it starts to dictate the way that you think, speak and act each moment. God's power will only follow our faith in His Word. He has promised that when we have faith in His Word, His power will always be there to back us up, and to demonstrate that what He has said is true (Jeremiah 1:12). When you have faith in His Word and begin to speak and act upon it, you will always see the miraculous follow. Everything we see was created by His Word, and as new creatures in Christ (2 Corinthians 5:17) we have the power and authority to activate that creative power into our atmosphere each and every moment.

I know that your Church may have never told you these things that I am telling you, but no pastor can deny that what I am saying is in God's Word. I don't care if your collar is turned around backwards or if you have a degree hanging on your wall, God's Word takes precedence. His wisdom is always revealed in His Kids. (Luke 7:35). You can believe and receive God's power given by His Word or you can doubt and do without.

Prayer: Dear Father God, thank you so much for making my heart leap and dance today by sharing your Holy Word with me. Thank you for promising to teach me Your Word each and every time I seek you for myself. Thank you for personally revealing yourself to me today so that I can rely on you and you alone through communion with your Holy Spirit. I believe and receive the truth and reliability of your Word and commit today to study it with a renewed excitement and energy that only your Spirit can provide. Amen!

GOSPILL 19

"Every word of God is pure: He is a shield unto them that put their trust in Him" (Proverbs 30:5).

I hope by now you are starting to see and experience the truth that is shown in God's Word. I believe that your spirit has been leaping on the inside of you as you see that you can rely on God and His Word as being the final authority in your life. My hope is that you see that God and His Word are *one*. You cannot separate God from His Word. When God sent Jesus to us, He sent His Word forth to us (John 1:14) in the form of a person. Jesus was, and is, literally the Word of God walking around. He first walked this earth in a skin suit led by the Holy Spirit, and today He still walks the earth on the inside of us believers, who share with Him in this same Spirit (1 Corinthians 6:17).

There is so much information today in this fallen world, but so little transformation. As the knowledge of this world seems to explode, the hearts of men seem to grow cold. The fire of the Holy Spirit is ignited in believers when they open up their hearts to His Holy Word and begin to hear The Words of The Master ringing in their ears each day. His still small voice encourages us, challenges us and empowers us to do the will (Word) of God as we sojourn on this earth as citizens of God's eternal kingdom. Yes, The Word of God is the final answer to all of life's challenging questions. We can pass the tests given to us each day, because God has given us the answer key—His Word.

God's Word will never fail you and will never leave you alone. Although the wisdom given to us by a loving parent or Grandparent is of great value, there is nothing like The Words of our heavenly Father spoken to us in our hearts each day. All you need is one dose of His Word each day to keep you healthy, joyful, and confident. I can assure you that as you begin to see the value of God's Word, you will begin to rely on it more and more, and soon you will be addicted to The Bread of Life and The Living Water that only Jesus can provide. God's only requirement for you to enjoy His bounty, is that you come to the dinner table hungry and thirsty (Matthew 5:6) each day and that you rely on Him to feed you with His goodness and mercy.

Prayer: Father God, thank you for inviting me to the table of the Lord Jesus Christ. Thank you for adopting me into the family of your dear Son Jesus and helping me to see that I can serve others with this same Love that you have shown me in Him. I go freely into this world today as a dispenser of your Grace and Mercy that you continue to lavish on me through Christ. As freely as I have received, freely today I give with a cheerful heart, knowing that I am pleasing to you as I walk in The Free Spirit of your beloved Son Jesus. In His name I pray. Amen!

GOSPILL 20

"As newborn babes, desire the sincere milk of the word that ye may grow thereby: If so be ye have tasted that the Lord is gracious" (1 Peter 2:2).

This passage helps us to see that God's Word is spiritual milk that helps our spirits to grow in Grace as we grow to know Jesus. As we grow to know Jesus and behold His beauty and wonder, we also see that He is slowly but surely transforming us into His image from glory to glory (2 Corinthians 3:18). His Word even says that when we are before Him one day we shall see Him for who He is, for we shall be like Him (1 John 3:2). We believers are like the moon; we have no light of our own, but we beautifully reflect the light of The Son. We give off a spiritual light that penetrates this darkened world, and when His light shines through us, darkness and fear have to flee and God's presence, His love, comes rushing in.

I love the fact that we have five senses in our Spirit that mirror the five senses that we have in our flesh. We can *now* taste and see that the Lord is good (Psalm 34:8) because God opens the eyes of our understanding (Ephesians 1:18) so that we can see and know Him better. He also tells us that we give off Christ's sweet fragrance in our Spirit (2 Corinthians 2:14) so that others can actually smell His presence on us. Also, our faith grows by hearing His Word (Romans 10:17); and He touches us with brotherly love so that we can touch others with the same love by His Spirit in us (1 Thessalonians 4:9).

Man, if you are not fired up by now on God's Word, your wood is wet! God wants you to know that His Word has to be the final authority in your life. If you were on the show Who Wants to Be a Millionaire, you could say that God's Word is your *final answer*. Peter encourages us to always be ready to give an answer for the hope that is in us (1 Peter 3:15), and he even refers to our hope found in Jesus as an "Anchor for our souls" (Hebrews 6:19). When we trust in God's Word He says we are like a tree planted by streams of living water (Psalm 1:3). He wants us to be rooted and grounded in His Love (Ephesians 3:17) so that we can grow in the rich soil of His Word and provide nourishment for hungry souls that enter our circle of grace.

Prayer: Father God, thank you for revealing The Truth of your Word in our spirit. Thank you for reconnecting us to The Vine (Jesus) so that we can grow as fruitful branches in your garden. Thank you for bringing us back to Eden to live in constant communion with you as you had originally intended. Thank you, Father, for the high privilege of moment by moment fellowship with you so that we can walk in your Word and thereby walk in your perfect Will. Amen!

GOSPILL 21

This verse clearly reveals once again that God's Word is activated by faith. I love the numerous times in The Gospels where Jesus commends those around him for activating their faith in Him. Faith is a free gift (Ephesians 2:8) given to us by God when we were born again into His Spirit. He commends us today for having faith in Him, and for using His faith to change our physical surroundings. I have seen even today many miracles activated by His faith through the Name of Jesus. In Jesus's name I prayed for my friend Joe's torn bicep to be healed, and God healed him instantly. I received an e-mail from a customer who was giving praise to God for answering our prayer. He needed to find a new home on very short notice, and The Lord led Him to a perfect place. Praise God! He hears and answers our prayers because He cares for us and for all of our needs (Philippians 4:19).

Jesus could do no mighty works until He was baptized by the Holy Spirit, and we today need Holy Spirit in us to make mountains move, to make cancer die and bodies and minds to be made whole. In the books of Acts (Acts 10:38) Jesus's brief three and a half year ministry is summed up by Peter when He says "Jesus of Nazareth went around doing good and healing ALL who were sick and oppressed by the devil." The Father (by way of Holy Spirit) has given us the same authority today by giving us the name of Jesus to identify ourselves and The Power to use His Name in faith to make the mountains of life move (Mark 11:22–24). Don't be afraid to exercise your authority today because when you see the manifestation of the Spirit of God, He gets all the glory, as it's only by Him doing these works through us that faith operates. We have the very same faith-filled spirit in us that raised Jesus from the dead (Ephesians 1:19), and we have been given His Name to use as the authority to back it up (Colossians 3:17).

Brothers and Sisters, I challenge you today to take a step of faith by getting out of the sinking boat (the world's system) and taking a step onto the water with Jesus. The Holy Spirit will lift you to new heights, of that you can be sure, but He will not lift you off of your couch. You have to take a step of faith knowing that He is behind you to back you up, and when you do, miracles will always follow. Don't be afraid, God has not given you the spirit of fear, but HAS instead given you His Power, His Love, and His Mind (2 Timothy 1:7). You are the one who decides how active God's power will become in your life and the lives of those around you.

Prayer: Father God, I come to you in the precious name of Jesus and thank you for giving me great boldness today! I am so excited about what we are going to do today. Amen.

GOSPILL 22

"Being born again, not of corruptible seed, but of incorruptible, by The Word of God, which liveth and abideth forever" (1 Peter 1:23).

Everything in this physical world is born from a seed, and creation goes on and on by the reproduction of seeds. In the Spiritual realm we are born again by the seed of God's Word. His Word is a seed that continues to replicate itself in the hearts/minds of believers. As we scatter the seed of The Word of God, faith comes alive and heaven is permitted to loose itself in the natural realm (Mark 4). Those who were destined to die to the sin of this natural world can be born again by hearing God's Word and receiving it into their heart as a seed that grows and grows throughout eternity (1 Peter 1:24–25). As we grow closer to God we rely more and more on the unseen world (His kingdom) and less and less on this world which is destined to fade away, as it is bound by time. God's Word/His seed is timeless (eternal) and not bound by time, but eternal, and those of us who receive Jesus as Lord are no longer shackled by time.

We have been made free from the corruption of this world and liberated into the glorious freedom of the children of God (Romans 8:21). We are actually born into this natural world with a sentence of death on our lives. The clock starts ticking at our natural birth, and we start the slow process of dying. Thanks be to God, when we are born again of the Spirit (simply by believing on Jesus) we are loosed from the cords of time and moved into an eternal state of fellowship with God (Romans 8). We now have the ability to pray the things of eternity (heaven) down to earth by speaking God's Word into this atmosphere of death, and we will always see His Spirit bring life and health to all who hear and receive by faith (Matthew 6:10 and Romans 4:17).

Faith is the bridge that brings the eternal state of heaven down to this dying world and faith is produced by hearing God's eternal Word (Romans 10:17). When we scatter the seed of God's Word into the hearts/minds of those around us, we can rest assured that one of two results will be produced:

people will be drawn in and changed or convicted and repelled. God's Word really is a two edged sword that cuts through all the BS and divides the things of eternity from the things of this world (Hebrews 4:12). We no longer swing a physical sword in battle like Saul did, but we swing the sword of God's Word by speaking it of our mouths (Romans 10:6–10). If this sounds crazy, just step over into the Spirit and get out of that fleshly body of death by renewing your mind to God's Word (Romans 12:2).

Prayer: Father God, thank you for showing me who I am in Christ. Thank you for showing me that I am united with you in one Spirit by faith and that I am heir to all that Christ has. Amen

GOSPILL 23

"He sent His Word, and healed them, and delivered them from their destructions" (Psalm 107:20).

When God sent Jesus to this earth, He sent the embodiment of His Word. Jesus is God's Word personified (John 1:1 and 1:14). Jesus shed His blood to cleanse the world of sin and was risen to heaven and seated at God's right hand where He remains today. For those of us who have made Him both Savior and Lord, He has sent His Holy Spirit to live in our hearts and to lead us and guide us like a Spiritual GPS (John 14:16–17). I guess you could say GPS stands for God's Positioning System. As believers today, we have the full authority of heaven here on earth and the matchless name of Jesus to back us wherever we go (Colossians 3:17). Both our words and our works are backed by The Power of God (Romans 1:16), and we are now able to perform the same works that Jesus performed while He walked the earth (John 14:12). You have all things that you need already in you by way of His Holy Spirit (2 Peter 1:3–4), and *you can do all things through Christ who stregnthens you* (Philippians 4:13).

I want you to go today into this dark world as His beloved child of light (Ephesians 5:6) and shine the light of the Lord on anyone who steps inside your circle (Matthew 5:14). God assures us that all people will know that we are called by Him and that they will have a reverence and an awe of His presence in us (Deuteronomy 28:10). God never sends His Kid's into unsafe places without first giving them the armor that they need to fight and win each and every battle (Ephesians 6:10). The only offensive weapon that He has given us in His arsenal is His Word which He calls His Sword. I like to say that S stands for Salvation and when you combine it with His Word you get SWord. Since this is a Spiritual battle, it is fought with words, and The Word takes precedence over every weak beggarly word that the devil has to offer. We believe and therefore we speak forth what God says and when we minister to others we minister with the power of His

Holy Spirit which always backs His Word (1 Peter 4:11).

You are a mighty child of God, who has been given fullness in Jesus Christ who is the head over all power and authority in heaven and on earth (Colossians 2:10). Don't call me crazy for saying this, I am just sharing His Word, and I share it because His Word Works! God's Word will *never* return void, but it will accomplish and prosper wherever you send it in prayer (Isaiah 55:11).

Prayer: Father, thank you for Jesus and His beautiful finished work on the cross. He died to make me righteous, and you promise that His righteousness is with me always and is making me bold like a lion (Proverbs 28:1). Thank you for bold Bible believing faith and the priceless name of Jesus to back it up where ever I go, whenever I need it! You are a good Dad and I love you. Amen!

GOSPILL 24

"Bless the Lord, ye His angels, that excel in strength, that do his commandments, hearkening unto the voice of His Word" (Psalm 103:20).

There is never a moment in your life when there are not angels ready, willing and able to move into your atmosphere and provide their strength and ability to drive away evil and fill you with praise. This verse makes it clear that what these ministering angels wait for is someone (you hopefully) to lend their voice to God's Word. His Word spoken on your lips has the same power and authority that it had on Jesus's lips when He walked this earth. "Speak Your Word only and my servant shall be healed" were the words of the Roman centurion who came to Jesus in hopes of seeing his dear servant healed and set free (Matthew 8:10). Jesus immediately commended this centurion, a heathen, for having greater faith than all of the modern *church* of that day! He loved the fact that the centurion had a revelation of how powerful His Words were. He knew that The Word of God could travel across continents and heal. A long walk to his servant's home was not needed, just a word from The Master.

Today, God has given us His Holy Spirit and encourages us in His Word to heal the sick, cleanse the lepers, and raise the dead by simply speaking His Word over ourselves and those around us in need (Matthew 10:8). I always like to say that He encourages us to turn our Matthew 8:10 (bold centurion faith) into a Matthew 10:8, where we speak His Word through the power of His Holy Spirit IN US (1 Peter 4:11). He encourages us to speak (with our mouth) three different times in Mark 11:23 and "SAY" to our mountains of difficulty, "Be thou removed and cast into the sea." When we speak this in faith we will see the Spirit of God move and our atmosphere change. This is 100 percent fact. You can believe and receive, or doubt and do without. I beg you at least to stop what you are doing right now and offer up a prayer of faith for yourself or someone that you know who is in need. Let that person know that you have prayed according to God's Word, and God has heard and answered and that they can expect their healing, deliverance, restoration, provision, etc. to come soon (Psalm 103:1–5). Let them know that Jesus gave you His Righteousness as a gift through His atonement and that He told you that the prayers of a righteous person are powerful and effective (James 5:15–16). This is not boasting in you, but boasting in the Lord who gave you His gift and His power when He gave you the Spirit of Christ to wear like a beautiful garment (Isaiah 61:10).

Prayer: Father God, I thank you and praise you for the free gift of Salvation found only in the matchless name of Jesus Christ my Lord. I thank you for your beautiful Holy Spirit that reveals Christ in me always by faith. I am so excited to be sharing this new life with you and I can't wait to see who crosses my path today because they are about to get blessed by God's best. Amen!

81

GOSPILL 25

"For whatsoever things were written aforetime were written for our learning, that we through patience and comfort of The Scriptures might have hope" (Romans 15:4–5).

I am so thankful that God has given me a copy of His Holy Word that I can look at and think about all day long. I cannot tell you the countless times that His Word has popped into my spirit when I was facing a trial or was just overjoyed by something wonderful. He has given us this hope (His Word) as an anchor for our souls (Hebrews 6:19). The Word of God is really active and alive (Hebrews 4:12) and gives us real patience, comfort, and hope as described in today's verse. Our only part is to open up His Word, and in so doing, open up the door of our heart to the Lord, and He will always be waiting on the other side to greet us and to fellowship with us.

I am so amazed that when Jesus came back from the dead and visited His disciples for forty days (He only visited believers) that He purposely kept them from recognizing Him in the flesh. The Bible says that on the road to Emmaus the two disciples walking with Jesus did not recognize Him by the outward man, that their eyes were *holden* (Luke 24:16) which means kept from seeing. As these two disciples walked and talked with the resurrected Lord they didn't know who He was. Instead of revealing Himself in the flesh, he spoke to their spirits by going through every Old Testament scripture that prophesied about His coming (Luke 24:27) and as He did this their hearts starting "burning within them" as He opened up the scriptures to them (Luke 24:32). This is such a beautiful picture of how the Lord intended for us to commune with Him *after* the cross. He intended from that day forward, that we use The Scriptures to communicate with Him and fellowship with Him, and He reminds us again and again that He *is one* with His Word. When you see Him in The Word, you see Him in your heart/spirit and as you behold Him in your heart you begin to think, talk, and act as He does. Yes, the Word of God is not something that can be contained, it is alive and living and infinite, and it is given to us as a free gift. As you read God's Word, He will speak to you heart to heart. As He speaks, you will grow closer to Him, and before you know it, you will begin to take on His character and nature (2 Corinthians 3:18).

Prayer: Father God, thank you for sending Jesus. Jesus, thank you for taking away my sins past, present, and future and sending me Your Holy Spirit to teach me each day. Thank you Holy Spirit for walking and talking with me every moment and revealing Christ in me to those who are lost, afraid, and lonely. Thank you, God, for helping me to see you through your Holy Word and for giving me revelation knowledge today that solidifies my faith in your Word. I believe that your Word is Truth and that today The Truth is setting me free. I am free to love others with the same unconditional love that you have for me. I am forgiven and free. Today I can fly like an Eagle above the wind and the waves and the cares of this world. Amen!

GOSPILL 26

"And many other signs truly did Jesus in the presence of His disciples, which are not written in this book: but these were written that you might believe that Jesus is the Christ, the Son of God: and that believing you might have life through His name" (John 20:30–31).

It's amazing that Jesus performed so many miracles in His brief three and a half year ministry that only some could be recorded. The scriptures say that if God were to try and record all of the miracles of Jesus that the world could not contain all of the books that would need to be written (John 21:25). If that doesn't excite you, then you need to get born again!

Today's scripture tells us another exciting truth, that these scriptures are given to us by God in order to create faith (Romans 10:17) which in turn allows us to cooperate with the divine Nature of God active in us through the Holy Spirit. The word "life" at the end of today's verse is translated from the Greek word Zoe, which means God's self-existent life. When we believe (exercise faith) through His Word we are partakers of God's divine nature, His very life. As believers, we have the same Spirit that raised Christ from the dead living in unison with our spirit. We are forever united in Spirit with God for the remainder of our lives on earth, and throughout eternity (2 Peter 1 and Ephesians 1:19). Sadly, most believers today live and die with The Power of God dormant on the inside of them. They simply die in ignorance due to their lack of knowledge of God's Word (Hosea 4:6).

I have good news for you today. If you have made Jesus your Lord and Savior, God *has given* you a new nature (2 Corinthians 5:17) by joining your spirit with His Holy Spirit. The purpose of this Spiritual operation is so that God can reveal to you who you are now in Christ. As you read and meditate on God's Word daily, you will begin to see (in your spirit) that you are God's beloved child (Romans 8:15) that you are a partaker of His divine nature (2 Peter 1:4) and that you can NOW do all things through Christ by walking in the Spirit (Philippians 4:13 and Galatians 5:25). From this day forward think of your Bible as a spiritual mirror that shows you what you are like on the inside. It reveals to you, moment by moment, day by day who you are in Christ and how God is slowly but surely transforming you (on the inside) into the very image of Jesus Himself (Romans 8:29). This is truly the Good News of the Gospel. I am sorry that they never taught you this in Sunday School, but I am confident that God's Spirit is revealing His truth to you right now, and faith is exploding on the inside of you. This is not just for super saints, this gift of God is for the weak and lowly, those humble enough to let go of the reigns and let God's Spirit take over and become your cruise control (2 Corinthians 4:7).

Prayer: Father God, thank you for the free gift of Salvation and for your presence in me constantly (24-7) through your Holy Spirit. I am so excited to walk and talk with you today as you lead me and guide me into this newness of life in the Spirit. You are wonderful! Amen!

GOSPILL 27

"For no matter how many promises God has made, they are 'Yes' in Christ. And so through Him the 'Amen' is spoken by us to the glory of God" (2 Corinthians 1:20).

I like to think of The Word of God as a Promise Book that God has given to His Children. I heard Billy Graham once say that there were over 10,000 promises to us in The Bible, and I have heard others say that the number is somewhere north of 3,000, and when I Googled this I came across the number 5,467. LOL! Today's verse makes me laugh because God is saying, hey whatever the real number is (and trust me He knows) that each and every promise is answered "Yes" in Christ. And since we are now hidden in The Body of Christ (Colossians 3:3) we can receive each and every promise by faith. Simply put, we can pray God's Word over each and every situation that life throws at us and see the manifestation of that promise here and now in this natural world. If you don't believe this, then I feel sorry for you because it won't work for you. His promises are manifested in the lives of believers and as I have said before, believers believe. It's who we are, it's what we do, we believe.

The Bible says that God has given us these great and precious promises (2 Peter 1:3–4) so that we can "partake of His divine nature" and escape the corruption of this world. Wow! These promises are given to us in the spiritual realm, and they are brought over to this natural world by a bridge called faith. Jesus says time and time again that our life will go the way of our faith, that things will happen to us in accordance with what we believe (Matthew 9:29). Job realized that the calamities that he faced were actually brought on by what he feared the most (Job 3:25); in other words, his fears were actually manifested in his life by what he believed. This is a great example of faith used for negative purposes. I believe that people who are sick, depressed, and without hope today are most often in those places because of their beliefs. Poverty itself is really just a mindset. Countless individuals have brought themselves out of poverty by seeing themselves as wealthy long before any real wealth was in their natural world. Simply put, faith works for either good or bad in your life, so why not believe for good?

I want to challenge you today to take one promise from God and write it on the palm of your hand so that you can see it throughout the day. I just wrote Philippians 4:13 on my hand which says, "I can do all things through Christ which strengthens me." God has promised that I am now one in Spirit with Christ (1 Corinthians 6:17) and by the power of His Spirit I can do all things. When I pray today for someone, I will pray in the Spirit and according to a promise of God that applies to each individual's situation, and God has promised to answer this prayer for Christ's sake and not our own (1 John 5:14–15). My confidence lies in Him and His promises, my hope is in His Word!

Prayer: Father God, thank you for showing me the truth of your precious Word today. Amen.

GOSPILL 28

"How sweet are your words to my taste, sweeter than honey in my mouth!" (Psalm 119:103).

Did you know that honey is the only food that doesn't perish? They have found honey in the ancient pyramids of Egypt that is over 4,000 years old, and it is just as fresh and tasty as the day it was made by God's bees. The Lord also reminds us that His Word is like honey, it tastes good to our spirit, and just like honey, it is actually good for our soul and body. He further reminds us that His Word never perishes or loses it's wonderful flavor when He says, "Heaven and earth will pass away, but my Words will never pass away" (Luke 21:33). He further reminds us that, "All men are like grass and all their glory like the flowers of the field, the grass withers and the flowers fall, but The Word of the Lord stands forever" (1 Peter 1:24–25).

My hope and prayer for you is that you are starting to see, hear, taste, smell, and feel that God's Word really is alive. Easter has recently passed, but the resurrected Spirit of Christ lives each and every day in your heart, and His resurrection life is raising you to new levels as you begin to experience the power of His Holy Word in your inward man. I believe that as you open your heart and mind each day to a new fresh Word from God, you are beginning to think and act like The Child of God that you are (Romans 8:16). God has placed His Spirit on the inside of you and promises you that He will never leave you nor forsake you (Hebrews 13:5). If God is with you and for you, then you should have no fear because He has your back 24/7 (Romans 8:31). The real good news is that His love for you is not based on your performance, but instead based on The Finished Work of Jesus Christ. Simply put, you will never be more righteous (in right standing with God), more loved, more blessed that you are right now at this very moment. I don't care what you have done, or how bad you think you are, God's love toward you is the very same love that He has for Jesus (John 17:23, 26), and this love is eternal. You are forever forgiven and forever free. Blessed are you because your sins and lawless deeds

He remembers *no more*, (Hebrews 8:12) and as far as the east is from the west (that's eternal distance) so far *has he* removed your sins from you (Psalm 103:12).

Prayer: Father God, thank you for sending Jesus to take my place on the cross so that I could be made forever right with you! Thank you for the perfect blood that was shed for me that makes me forever clean. All sin past, present, and future is removed, and I am clean before you because His work is finished. Thank you, God, for sending me your Holy Spirit so that I can understand who I am and what I have in Christ. I am your child, and as your child I can come to you, Dad, with confidence and boldness knowing that you love me and want what is best for me. I trust you to lead me and guide me today, Holy Spirit, so that I can bless someone in need. Jesus has set me free, and today I walk in that freedom that He purchased for me! Amen.

GOSPILL 29

"My covenant will I not break, nor alter the thing that is gone out of my lips" (Psalm 89:34).

God said it, we believe it, and that settles it! As the Holy Spirit begins to reveal to you that His Word is truth (John 17:17) you begin to start thinking and talking like Jesus himself. There is nothing more pleasing to The Father than to hear His children speak out His Words of wisdom over their own lives and the lives of their loved ones. His Word says that our tongue is like the pen of a ready writer (Psalm 45:1). As we speak His Word into the atmosphere here on earth we can literally bring the things of heaven down and see His kingdom grow (Matthew 6:10).

When we look at the life of Jesus in the Gospels, we see that He was always reciting God's Word into the atmosphere as he went about doing good and healing ALL who were oppressed by the devil (Acts 10:38). We are called to do no less today. Jesus has given us the promised Holy Spirit and His Word, and he commands us to lay hands on the sick and see them be made well (Matthew 10:8). He has promised us that because God (Holy Spirit) is always with us, we ALWAYS have His power to back His Word and His Name. Oh, the beautiful name of Jesus on your lips has such power and authority! He died to make it so! Jesus even promised us that we would be able to perform the exact same mighty works that He did and even greater works (John 14:12). Jesus is now at the Father's right hand interceding for us in prayer and communicating to us through the Holy Spirit as we go through this life walking in His faith.

The Church today is living so far below the poverty line when it comes to operating in faith and in the power of the Holy Spirit. Jesus could do no mighty works until he received the baptism of the Holy Spirit, and we believers today must rely also on the same Spirit and anointing. I urge you today to ask God to reveal the Holy Spirit in you, and I implore you to welcome Holy Spirit into your heart. Ask Him to take the reins and lead you and guide you as you go about your day. The first thing the enemy will try to do is convince you that you don't have (and can never have) the Holy Spirit. I want to assure you today that God is more desirous to give you His Holy Spirit than you are to receive Him (please see Luke 11:13). Please know that Holy Spirit is ready, willing, and able to work through you right now in the name of Jesus!

Prayer: Father, I recognize my need for Your power to live this new life. Please fill me with your Holy Spirit. By faith I receive Him right now. Thank you for baptizing me. Holy Spirit, you are welcome in my life. Amen!

GOSPILL 30

"In the beginning was the Word, and the Word was with God, and the Word was God" (John 1:1).

Congratulations on taking your final dose of God's thirty day prescription of His Word! Hopefully by now you are becoming fully convinced that God's Word is life (Zoe) and health to all of your mind and body (Proverbs 4:22). Hopefully by now you have experienced your spirit leaping and dancing inside you as the truth of God's Word quickens your mortal body. His Word has such great power when you allow it into your life through your free will. I hope these daily doses of God's Word have given you a greater hunger for His Word so that you can boldly come to Him each morning for a complete breakfast.

I chose today's verse (I had help) because it shows us, once again, that God and His Word cannot be separated. His Word is the essence of who He is. If you want to see what His Word looks like in action, just look to Jesus who was God's Word in human flesh (John 1:14). The Father makes it very clear that Jesus is the exact representation of who He is (Hebrews 1:3). He is a perfect picture of what The Word of God looks like when you put hands and feet to it by faith (Colossians 1:15). Jesus Himself reminded His disciples that when they were looking at Him, they were looking at The Father (John 14:7).

Sometimes we make the mistake of thinking that it would be great if we could just see Jesus here in person. We think that nothing could be better than to have Him sitting here with us in the flesh so we could see Him, hear Him, and talk with Him. Jesus promised us that He gave us something better when He ascended into heaven (John 16:7). When He finished His work He ascended up to heaven and was seated at The Father's right hand. His finished work has allowed Him to send the Holy Spirit to anyone who has accepted Him as Lord and Savior. This is such a better deal because now you have Jesus with you 24/7, and there is *never* a time when He is not with you (Hebrews 13:5). He is an ever present help in times of trouble (Psalm 46:1). He sits next to The

Father and intercedes for us in prayer when we aren't sure how to pray or what to say (Romans 8:26). Isn't it wonderful that we share the same heart/spirit with Jesus, and He knows already what we need before we even ask (Psalm 139)? I can't think of anything more reassuring than knowing Jesus is speaking to The Father on my behalf, especially when my prayers seem muted.

Prayer: Jesus, thank you for taking residence in my heart and for being with me always. Amen!

Closing thoughts: I hope you have enjoyed this thirty day dose of God's Word that I am affectionately referring to as Gospills. My hope is that these past thirty days have been a time of rest and refreshing and that the Holy Spirit has quickened the truth of God's Word to you, and that your faith has increased to new heights. I encourage you to stay in God's Word every day, and I pray that God will move you up heaven's ladder as you grow in grace and in the knowledge of the Lord Jesus Christ. May His presence, His Word, dwell in you richly by faith and may His power be made manifest in your life as you begin to speak and act on His Holy Word. He is with you always and for you always. He calls you His friend and so much more.

Yours in Christ, Jeff Johnson.

Please visit us at www.gospills.com to sign up for our free daily devotional or to send a Gospill to a friend or loved one.

ABOUT THE AUTHOR

Jeff Johnson is a passionate follower of Jesus Christ who loves to share his enthusiasm for God's Holy Word with fellow believers and seekers alike.

By trade, Jeff is director of sales for a generic drug manufacturer based in Mumbai, India.

Jeff is also a volunteer chaplain at Florida State Prison where he often visits and encourages his brothers in blue. His ministry has a special emphasis on the wonderful benefits that believers can experience through the discipline of daily devotional time with the Lord.

Jeff has been married to his beautiful wife, Kathleen, for twenty-one years. They share their home in Ponte Vedra Beach, Florida, with their sixteen-year-old daughter Kendall and their three cats: Rosie, Dandelion and Finn.

Jeff's second book *Gospills vol 2* (Being Thankful Is Good Medicine) is also available wherever books are sold.

You may contact Jeff at
Web: www.Gospills.com
Email: Gospills@aol.com